T0193336

PAY IT FORWARD GUIDE

INSPIRED BY PAY IT FORWARD HEARTS

KRISTI ARNO

BALBOA.
PRESS
A DIVISION OF HAY HOUSE

Balboa Press books may be ordered through booksellers or by contacting:

Balboa Press
A Division of Hay House
1663 Liberty Drive
Bloomington, IN 47403
www.balboapress.com
1 (877) 407-4847

Print information available on the last page.

ISBN: 978-1-9822-0279-8 (sc)
ISBN: 978-1-9822-0281-1 (hc)
ISBN: 978-1-9822-0280-4 (e)

Library of Congress Control Number: 2018904957

Balboa Press rev. date: 05/11/2018

Kristi Arno

Inspired by Pay It Forward Hearts

CONTENTS

PART 1: COMPASSION OUTREACH

PART 2: KINDNESS CHALLENGE

DEDICATION

To my husband, my partner, my friend. You are without a doubt my God wink from above. Your love and constant positive encouragement has been instrumental into turning my thoughts, ideas, and passion into a realization. Thank you just doesn't seem enough.

I would also like to express my deepest gratitude to my family and friends who have been tremendously supportive. Your unwavering love has meant the world to me and given me the courage to venture off the well-worn path. Thank you from the bottom of my heart.

INTRODUCTION

If you persevere through your struggles, then you tend to uncover your strength, or in my case I was guided towards my life's purpose. This book originated from a chapter in my life where I was at my lowest. My unexpected purpose was birthed out of a darkness, a state of depression, someplace I would possibly categorize as rock bottom. However, I learned my most treasured lesson at rock bottom; If you need a miracle become a miracle for someone else. When you take time investing in others, the seeds you sow will certainly make its way back to you much like a boomerang. The energy you put out into the universe, be that positive or negative, unquestionably is returned. What I needed most during this dark time in my life was love, grace, and compassion. So, in turn, this is what I would flood the world with. To pull myself out of darkness with my new mission, I formed a volunteer group consisting of family and friends and our primary focus was to Pay It Forward to others.

Pay it Forward means to do a random act of kindness for another in hopes that it touches the receiver's heart and they in turn continue to pass on the kindness to others. Our intent is to reach out to those who might need an encouraging word to keep moving forward. Support from strangers does wonders for both the volunteers and those on the receiving side of love. When you spend time with those in trying situations, you find you are not alone. Often times you discover your situation does not even compare to what others are going through and it's with this revelation that your heart opens with compassion and healing for your own situation. With the outreach activities, our non-profit's hope is to create a ripple effect of kindness throughout our streets, zip codes, cities, states, and eventually the world.

Out of my struggles came this volunteer group which evolved into its own non-profit and now the idea of this book. Many pay it forward ideas can be found on websites and internet blogs. However, this book is intended to guide in basic ideas, preparation, planning, and organization for outreach events. This is not an all-inclusive, but it can help in providing ideas on how to coordinate and organize your outreach activities. With this information, you too can spread kindness in your community focusing on supporting specific outreach groups or by taking the personal Pay It Forward challenge.

By joining together and spreading love, we can change the trajectory of the world one random act of kindness at a time.

PART 1

COMPASSION OUTREACH

CHAPTER 1

Homeless Outreach

It was the middle of October in Kansas, my absolute favorite time of year. When the trees scream autumn with red, orange, and yellow tinted leaves falling to the ground. Pumpkin flavored everything; coffee, hand soaps, candles, desserts, you name it. The weather is perfect for sweaters, comfy jeans, and boots while attending football games and bonfires outdoors surrounded by family and friends. To make it even sweeter, my fiancé, Dan, and I were in the middle of brainstorming locations for our upcoming wedding.

Early in our relationship, we were big concert goers and would often walk downtown by this picturesque park on our way to the events. He suggested this park as a venue for our wedding and I instantly agreed this was the perfect location. This midtown park is scenic and beautiful with large mature trees, a quaint gazebo, and a small tranquil bridge over a very desolate stream surrounded with large rocks to enclose the parameter of the park. We both had been married before and weren't looking for a big to-do wedding. This was the perfect location for our ceremony. One small detail was brought to our attention, this is a common hangout for homeless in the community.

This could have been a problem; however, a bucket list item of mine was to feed the homeless; I thought what better time than this! Let's do it! Let's incorporate the homeless into our wedding day. After some brainstorming, we decided to serve the homeless lunch in lieu of a wedding reception that day. At first our parents were shocked. I believe the exact response by all was, "You want to do what? Are you serious?!" We were absolutely serious, this was a perfect way to start our journey together.

To get everyone involved, we turned it into a family affair. The night before our wedding day, Dan, our parents and myself all went to the grocery store together to buy our food for the next day. After much discussion, we decided to serve peanut butter and jelly sandwiches and bologna sandwiches for the main course. We agreed they both have a good protein and carbohydrate balance which is important. Now which condiments? When it comes to bologna sandwiches, some prefer mayo others prefer mustard. To solve the dilemma, we went with both. The ladies took to the cookie aisle and carefully selected treats that would be enjoyed by everyone. The men went in search for water and chips to create a diverse yet filling meal. Lastly, my Dad thought what better way to celebrate than with cigars! We threw that into the basket too! After an hour at the store, we retreated to my parent's house and gathered around the kitchen island. We began preparing, packaging, and getting organized for our outreach activity the next day. This became a fun coming together of families in what could have been a stressful wedding preparation time!

The next day was a beautiful Wednesday in October for Kansas. The weather was sunny and in the mid 70's with little to no breeze. In fact, it was the last lovely day of the year. Surely no coincidence. We had important work to be done. First a ceremony that would bond Dan and me together for life, then a family outreach activity that would ignite a path neither of us knew we were being led down. Nine of us gathered in jeans for our brief exchange of vows; Dan's parents, my parents, and two of our church Pastors. I was calm and peaceful, ready for our lives to be officially joined as one. In this moment, I had no idea the impact this day would have on my life and the path it would lead me down. It was life changing.

Once our short ceremony finished, we retreated to the vehicles to get the food we prepared. We laid out the premade sandwiches, cookies, chips, and water on the park benches to begin serving our meal. The homeless men and women came from miles around once the word was out food was being served in the park. Our parents and Pastors mingled with the 50+ homeless and everyone was smiling and enjoying the coming together of community. The gratitude and appreciation being expressed by the group was palpable. Suddenly, it clicked with our parents. "I get it now! I get why you wanted to do this!" they exclaimed.

There is no greater feeling than helping those around you. When you reach out and help those in need you feel a sense of joy and happiness that can't be purchased by material possessions or accolades. Just knowing you have helped another human being in their moment of need, creates a sense of awareness and compassion that allows you to recognize a world outside of yourself. For a moment, you get out of your own bubble, your own worries, and acknowledge the struggles of those around you. With this new-found awareness, you tend to lead a happier, gentler, more peaceful life because you have a deep seeded understanding that everyone has difficulties. Reaching out to help others is the most basic level of kindness and love you can give another human being.

Lending a hand to the homeless in your community is much easier than you think. Homeless lack the necessities which most of us take for granted every day; such as a roof over your head, a cleansing shower, brushing your teeth, a bed to sleep in, water to drink, and food on your plate. A common misconception made is linking homelessness with the characteristics of laziness, alcoholism and or drug addiction. With this perception the last thing people want to do is interact and certainly not create a relief or support. In my experience, often homeless people fell to this level due to a series of bad luck which spiraled out of control and led them to this unfortunate situation. A life changing crisis such as divorce, substance abuse, untreated mental illness, and loss of a job all are contributors to homelessness. Their intention was never to fall this far from grace, but life happened.

My hope is if I were in this situation where contributing factors led me to be without a roof over my head and food in my belly, someone would be kind enough to reach out and help me. No judgements - just help me. It's my responsibility to get my feet back on the ground. However, support from your local community is instrumental in encouraging recovery and rebound from such dark places.

To lend a hand, coordinating a drive to collect donations is easy and can be done with a group of friends, family, neighborhood, church groups, community groups, schools, and on individual levels. Often, the entire family can join together with this outreach activity as children could participate with parental approval and supervision. Safety is always important so be aware of your surroundings and always volunteer in a group setting. Often times because they are at a point in their lives where they have nothing, they are overwhelmingly grateful and want to express their love by giving a hug to show their appreciation. If you do not feel comfortable, merely shake their hand and continue on with the conversation. Remember they are people too.

Reach out to your local non-profits who support local shelters and homeless outreach activities to see how you can help. Often, they rely on donations from the community in which case you could coordinate a drive to help replenish essential items.

Preparing for a Homeless Outreach:

Homeless feedings can be organized on an individual basis or with a group of like-minded people. Make a list of food items you would like to serve and divide amongst your volunteers to purchase. Remember, often times there is not an adequate meal setting in the location of the homeless, so keep it simple and easy to prepare and transport. Do not complicate with added condiments or liquids. Do as much prep work before hand to make the actual feeding simple. Basic meals such as pre-assembled sandwiches, takeout pizza, and hamburgers and/or hotdogs are popular items to serve. Takeout pizza is as easy as simply ordering and delivering to the location. Hamburgers or hotdogs will need to be cooked prior and kept warm unless you are bringing a grill along to the serving. Sandwiches are also easy to prepare and transport.

A menu example could be to prepare the bologna sandwiches ahead of time and place in individual sandwich bags. Purchase cookies and place 4-5 in individual sandwich bags or purchase prepackaged snack size. Also, an assortment of 1.5-ounce single serving potato chips are popular items. By doing this, the process is easy and quick as you set all the food in a cafeteria style layout and create a line when serving (see example below). Volunteers are needed in preparing the food, transporting the food, and serving the food.

Sample menu of food items for homeless feeding. Determine the amount to purchase based on the approximate number of people attending the feeding.

- ☐ Grocery bags for food
- ☐ Sandwich Bags

☐ Loaves of bread

☐ Peanut Butter & Jelly

☐ Bologna

☐ 1.5-ounce single serving potato chips

☐ Crackers or Granola bars

☐ Cookies or snack size prepackaged cookies

☐ Fruit (bananas, apples, oranges)

☐ Bottled water

The manner in which you organize the setup of food is important for ease of flow when serving. Below is an example of how to layout your menu. Have a volunteer at each station serve their assigned item, as this makes your outreach more personable and heartfelt. After all, your team personally made this meal; you want them to know you care and you want the volunteers to see their love in action.

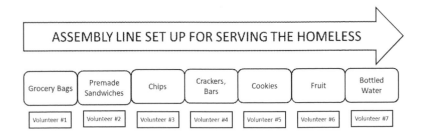

Assembling care packages:

Care packages are great for a group outreach activity and creates a sense of teambuilding and comradery. First, coordinate the purchasing of essential items you want to provide (see recommended list at the end of this chapter). Ask for volunteers to purchase the items on your list. Once you have all the items being assembled, organize items by categories i.e travel size toiletries, snacks, etc. Next, create an assembly line and assign each volunteer(s) a station they are responsible for packaging. A good deal of work can be accomplished in a short amount of time with lots of volunteers and organizing the layout effectively. Once all the care packages are assembled, they can be donated to non-profits or delivered directly to individuals in need.

Below is an example of items that could be packaged together into separate sandwich bags by volunteers:

Volunteer Team 1 - Bag 1

- ☐ Travel size shampoo/conditioner
- ☐ Travel size body wash/bar soap

- ☐ Travel size lotion
- ☐ Toothbrush/toothpaste
- ☐ Hair brush

Volunteer Team 2 - Bag 2

- ☐ Chap stick
- ☐ Kleenex
- ☐ Feminine products
- ☐ Sunscreen
- ☐ Antibacterial wipes

Organizing a Donation Drive:

Donation drives can be used to collect anything from clothing, bicycles, shoes, sleeping bags, or pre-filled backpacks with emergency items. Spread the word to your local churches, schools, companies, or community clubs that you are having a drive to collect specific items for the homeless and indicate a specific drop off location. Don't forget to utilize social media and fliers to market your need. The flyer should include what items you are requesting, who will benefit from their donations, when you need them by, and where to drop them off. Be sure to include a specific deadline so people know when you expect to collect the items. When sorting through the donations, have a sizable number of volunteers to help sort and organize, if not, this task can be daunting. Donation drives take time since you first must get the word out, then collect, sort and lastly distribute. However, the reward is very heartfelt by all.

Timeline:

- ✓ Identify your purpose for the drive. What need are you hoping to help?
- ✓ Once you know what it is you are collecting, reach out to local nonprofits to determine who could benefit most from your donations.
- ✓ Get the word out by social media, flyers, websites, newspapers, or TV. It's important to include which organizations will be receiving the donations.
- ✓ Set up collection bins at your identified drop off stations.
- ✓ Collect donations periodically throughout your drive. This avoids stolen or over full bins.

- ✓ Once the drive is finished collect all donations in one central location.
- ✓ Have volunteers help sort through the donations and categorize appropriately, as needed.
- ✓ Coordinate a good time to deliver donations to their respective locations.

Feeding using leftover food from events:

If you attend a social function and have left over food consider taking it to your local homeless community. Anything from excess hamburgers/hotdogs, sandwiches, pizza, cupcakes could be donated to those in need. If you own a restaurant, you could reach out to your local non-profits and see if they could make use of the leftover daily food not able to be served in the restaurant.

Restaurant Style Serving:

Rent out a local community building and serve a meal as that from a restaurant. Ideally, provide something easy to prepare and serve quickly, such as soup, chili, sandwiches, pizza, or hotdogs and hamburgers. Allow the homeless to come in, be seated and treated as if they were in a restaurant setting. This takes much more planning and logistical preparation. However, if done correctly, it will be a spectacular event for the homeless.

Essential items to be collected and donated for the described homeless activities are as follows, but not limited to:

- ☐ Travel size shampoo
- ☐ Travel size conditioner
- ☐ Toothbrush
- ☐ Toothpaste
- ☐ Chap Stick
- ☐ Hairbrush
- ☐ Body Wash
- ☐ Bar Soap
- ☐ Anti-bacterial wipes
- ☐ Feminine products
- ☐ Socks
- ☐ Shoes (tennis shoes, flip flops, boots, dress shoes)
- ☐ Blankets
- ☐ Bottled Water
- ☐ Sunscreen

- ☐ Sleeping bag
- ☐ Clothing items
- ☐ Fruit (bananas, apples, oranges, etc)
- ☐ Nuts
- ☐ Beef Jerky
- ☐ Granola bars
- ☐ Cereal
- ☐ Gift certificates to fast food restaurants
- ☐ Feet/hand warmers
- ☐ Tissues/Kleenex
- ☐ Winter wear (hats, gloves, stocking caps, coats, sweat shirts)
- ☐ First Aid Items
- ☐ Backpacks

CHAPTER 2

Women's Shelter

Ever since I can remember, I wanted to volunteer at our local battered women's shelter. I felt drawn to this specific cause due to events in my childhood and wanted to help these women in some way. The women who escape from abusive circumstances are burdened with concerns of where they will live, where will they get their income for food, shelter, and most of all, where will they be safe. Those with children have the added pressure of keeping their children safe while trying to keep the days as normal as possible for these precious, innocent victims.

With that said, this was one of our first "Pay it Forward" events as a non-profit. We wanted to "celebrate" the ladies of the shelter by serving a warm brunch in a party themed atmosphere. Fast approaching was Valentine's Day, a popular commercialized holiday which celebrates the relationship between significant others, and/or their children. Our timing was perfect! Husbands, wives, or significant others shower their mate with flowers, chocolates, candy, and romantic greeting cards to show their love and affection on this day. What the women at the battered shelters are overcoming is the furthest from feelings of love, caring, acceptance, warmth, and unconditional love from a significant other. The purpose of our event was to spread support and encouragement to them and their children on this commercialized day. This is why I felt it was imperative we celebrate this specific holiday with them, Valentine's Day.

In preparing for the event, I took to planning the details of this party as though it was for myself. What would I want if I were in their shoes? What would make me feel loved and appreciated? What would make me feel like a special woman? What would take my mind off my situation even for just a few hours? With these answers, the planning began. We ordered festive balloons to hang throughout the kitchen hall, red, white, and pink decorations to cover each of the tables, roses throughout the room, fun upbeat party songs to blast in the background, warm homemade food baking in the kitchen, a kids table with grab bags and fun finger food such as pop tarts, Rice Krispy treats, and festive cupcakes. A gifting of a stuff the purse activity where participants were able to pick a gently used, donated, designer purse of their choosing and fill it with beauty products. Our hope is this would help them replenish what items they might have left behind as they left their situation urgently. We were also able to partner with a local spa to provide eyebrow waxing for the women and shellac manicures for the younger girls. Such a lovely Valentine's Day event; warm food, celebration, shopping, and being pampered!

For me as the event coordinator, my job is to manage and oversee the event from beginning to end. I plan all the details with the non-profit before the day, confirm we have enough volunteers, ensure we have enough donated items for the event, assign everyone jobs to their liking, and make sure everyone (volunteers and those we are serving) are feeling the generosity and love that brings us together. It's easy to get lost in the madness of the event. However, the whirlwind at this particular event came to an immediate stop when a lady in her twenties came up to me and stopped me dead in my tracks. She put both her hands holding the upper part of my arms to get my attention. She said, "I really want to thank you for today." I said in passing, "Oh sure, absolutely, no problem" and proceeded to swiftly move past her. Women are not great at accepting compliments. We tend to deflect and make light of admiring comments as though we are not worthy of such praise. I believe we are more comfortable that way, not right, but comfortable. She then jerked both my arms as to get my attention more intently. She looked me straight in the eyes until our eyes connected. I now could see her, really see her. Her eyes were welt up with tears about to skate down her face. She said, "No, really, thank you so much for today. You have no idea what this means to us. Your group coming here, supporting us, thank you." In that moment, I stopped and acknowledged the feedback. I felt the chills in that moment. We had made a difference! Just as we hoped. I gave her a hug with a squeeze that was tight with intent. Her comments were a sign from God that these ladies felt loved, felt supported. Our goal was to help them dig deep and find the courage within themselves to put one foot in front of the other in pursuit of a healthier life for themselves and their children. That day was a success. They walked away knowing strangers do care.

According to domesticshelters.org more than 1 in 3 women in the USA have experienced some form of domestic violence. This statistic is alarming and hits close to home for many households. If you have not personally been a victim of domestic violence statistics would conclude someone in your life has; such as your mother, your sister, your niece, your cousin, your friend, your neighbor or your co-worker. The mental abuse that is layered upon the physical abuse makes it extremely difficult for one to leave the unhealthy environment. The abuser has manipulated the woman into thinking she is not able to survive without them. And in some cases, made the victim believe she has brought on the physical or mental abuse herself by actions she's done or not done. This is simply not true. No person deserves to be treated in such a way. Women attempt to leave an average 7 times before they remove themselves from the situation according to Stand for Families Free of Violence website, www.standffov.org. It takes an enormous amount of courage to leave a situation permanently and not return.

What can we do to help support and encourage women who have mustered up the courage to leave such a situation? Below are some ways to show support, encouragement, and love to those who are at their most vulnerable state.

Stuff the purse:

Women often leave abusive situations urgently and are not able to take a great deal with them. They tend to leave with what they are wearing and can carry because it's about survival and removing themselves from the dangerous situation. This means they leave behind the daily rituals of getting ready each day such as, shampoo/conditioner/soaps for showering, lotions, and makeup. One idea on how to pamper the women of the shelter is a stuff the purse event. Request donations of a variety of gently used designer purses from your community as well as unused makeup, body lotions, face creams, nail polish, jewelry, feminine products, and shampoo and conditioner. Women tend to accumulate more beauty products than they need or use so this is a wonderful opportunity to ask for donated beauty items. I have found women are happy to donate their unused beauty products for this cause as women understand the importance of feeling good about yourself.

The way you organize and display the setup of items is important for ease of shopping for handbags and beauty items. To create a stuff the purse theme, display the donated handbags on a table followed by the donated beauty products. Allow the women to select a purse (or purses depending on the amount donated) and go through the beauty products and stuff the purse full of goodies.

Below is an example of how to layout your "Stuff the purse" event. If you'd like, have a volunteer at each station help the women select the beauty products, as this makes your outreach more personable and heartfelt.

It's important to have your volunteer's hands on showing their love in action.

Brunch:

Depending on the funds the non-profit receives, the shelters often serve cold food to their residents such as cereal, pastries and toast for breakfast. Organizing a warm brunch can be a heartfelt treat for the women and a personal touch they are lacking. Before planning your menu, first visit or ask the shelter what size kitchen they have. With a full-size kitchen including a stove, microwave, and warmers the food items can be made freshly onsite. If they have a limited kitchen, stick to easier food items or prepare the food in advance and transport in crockpots or warmers. If you are bringing in personal cooking items such as utensils, bowls, crock pots, etc. it is recommended to mark them in some manner so they are easily identified as yours. Confirm with the non-profit you are supporting, if they require volunteers to have a Food Handlers Card. An easy way to incorporate volunteers not having a Food Handlers Card is to have shifts of volunteers responsible for different activities to help spread responsibilities.

A sample of volunteer shifts are below. Evaluate each task and assign the number of volunteers appropriately for your specific event.

- ✓ Team of volunteers to coordinate the donation and transportation of food the day of event.
- ✓ Team of volunteers (with Food Handling Cards) to cook and serve the food.

✓ Team of volunteers to act as the cleanup crew to wash dishes and tidy up the space after the event. Keep in mind the cleanup will take longer if you are not using disposable items.

Sample menu for battered women brunch. Determine the amount to purchase based on the approximate number of people attending the brunch.

☐ Scrambled Eggs

☐ Microwavable Bacon or Sausage

☐ Pancakes or frozen waffles

☐ Premade Potato Casseroles

☐ Fruit

☐ Juice

☐ Condiments (butter, syrup, etc.)

☐ Paper plates, utensils, napkins

☐ Plastic gloves

☐ Alternative accommodations for those with allergens

Spa day:

Partnering with a local spa to create a pampering day

for the ladies is something they will never forget. When planning such an activity, first check with the shelter and see how many women would be participating. With the right number of Nail Technicians and Estheticians, waxing and manicures can be easily performed on a number of women in a reasonable amount of time. Once you have the number of women participating, coordinate with the Spa Manager, Esthetician, and Nail Tech for logistics and amount of time for each service so you can plan accordingly. Ensure the Spa Manager has each woman receiving a treatment complete a medical waiver as they would clients in their own Spa. This is to ensure safety for the clients as well as the Spa. Or if you are not partnering with a spa, provide your own variety of nail polishes, warm towels and mani/pedi tools and have the ladies do their own manicures and pedicures on each other. Find a quiet area/room in the shelter and setup with a spa theme. Soft relaxing music which can be downloaded from a free app, aromatherapy diffuser to create a calming smell and warm towels are just a few small touches that create an easy spa like theme.

Dinner and Movie night:

Pizza, popcorn, and movie night is something easy and simple to organize. Determine the amount of pizza needed for the evening and order appropriately. Select a funny upbeat movie that would appeal to all ages. Laughter is the best medicine so funny comedy movies are the best choice. If children will be present, consider showing the most recent popular animated movie. Balloons and cupcakes are a great way to liven up the evening and make it a fun party atmosphere. If a microwave is available, popcorn is a wonderful added touch.

Holiday Theme Party:

Consider a holiday themed party with the shelter. Any of the above ideas can be combined in a themed party atmosphere. Celebrating holidays such as Valentine's Day, Mother's Day, Thanksgiving, and Christmas are added touches because they are away from their family and friends during the time of transition. This is also just as important for their children who are feeling the separation of what they knew life to be like. It's a thoughtful added touch of remembering them on such monumental holidays. This encouragement is most important as they are starting a new fresh uncertain life.

Craft Day:

If you have craft skills consider spending an afternoon with the ladies to pass on your knowledge. Wheat weaving, jewelry making, cards and baking can all be organized with the proper amount of inventory and tools provided. Consult an experienced volunteer to advise the amount of inventory and time needed before pursuing.

Reach out to your local women's shelter non-profits to see what items they are in need of. Essential items which could be donated are as follows, but not limited to:

- ☐ Shampoo / Conditioner
- ☐ Body Wash
- ☐ Bar Soap
- ☐ Lotions
- ☐ Feminine Products
- ☐ Unused Makeup
- ☐ Deodorant
- ☐ Bra

- ☐ Underwear
- ☐ Socks
- ☐ Dress clothes
- ☐ Handbags
- ☐ Shoes
- ☐ Gift Cards

CHAPTER 3

Community Clean Up

It was a scorching, bright, summer July day in Kansas. At twelve years old, I was a blonde haired, awkward pre-teenage girl with braces just entering junior high. My church youth group had coordinated an activity to pick up trash along the local river as a community outreach activity. With a black trash bag in hand, I went on my way picking up whatever debris had washed up along the shoreline after our recent city festival; empty soda cans, beer bottles, candy wrappers, potato chip bags, pizza boxes, and even some worn clothing. I recall laughing with my girlfriend as we enjoyed ourselves that day picking up trash and calling it undiscovered treasures. It was a sweltering hot day, so hot that on our adventure we came across several black snakes sunbathing along the rocks by the river. We first screamed uncontrollably and ran away making a ruckus. We were half scared and half enjoying the thrill. Even with the heat and excitement, it was a good day. I may only have been twelve years old, but I was beginning to understand no matter what age you are, you can help and give back to your community. I wasn't even old enough to drive, barely had hair on my legs, no boyfriend yet, and here I was helping beautify my city. The simple act of picking up trash instills a sort of ownership and pride about your community. Never again would I throw something out the window without regard for a trash can and not recall this day. The effort of dozens to pick up trash left behind by others helps you immediately respect the property around you.

What I realized as I grew older is this experience would stick with me for the rest of my life. From that point forward, I would crave the feeling of helping others. Similar to how dopamine effects the brain when a teenager has their first hit off a cigarette, alcohol or drug and then the child desires more of the substance;

my brain was reacting the same way but to community service. I was experiencing what is known as a helpers-high which spurs a feed-good chemical after one does a good deed. Participating in community outreach activities, at such a young age built the foundation of desire to help others. I would remember this day and how it made me feel electrified inside, happy, fulfilled, purposeful, impactful and would want to duplicate these feelings. While riding my bike throughout our city I would come across a homeless person and want to bring them bread and water. Or I would see trash in a parking lot and go out of my way to pick it up and dispose of it properly. Or return an abandoned shopping cart to its rightful location. The feeling of helping others and giving back had been introduced to me at a young age and from that day forward, I wanted to help others. As I became an adult, I would understand the significance of the ripple effect serving others does for your community as well as yourself. No matter how small the act of kindness you do, it is worth doing.

Cleaning up your city is an easy community outreach activity anyone can participate in. It can be an enjoyable teambuilding experience for families, friends, employers, Boy Scouts, Girl Scouts, church groups, Greek organizations, book clubs, or other social and volunteer organizations. Not a great deal of preparation or items are required and it's fun for all ages. If kids are participating, it is important to have parental supervision and permission. It's imperative to have enough adults to monitor all the children always. Most school systems suggest that one adult be present for every 8 to 10 students. Proper clothing attire is essential such as comfortable walking shoes. Also, depending on the time of year, sunscreen, bug spray, and hydration since the activity is usually all outdoors.

Reach out to your local Chamber of Commerce to find out if there is a community group you can join or if there are laws around community beautification. Also, inquire about prime areas in need of clean up, and when is an opportune time trash pickup is needed, maybe after a city festival or outdoor concert.

One effortless way to do a clean-up in a parking lot or large field is what is known as a FOD line (Foreign Object Debris line). Everyone stands in a line and walks the area together picking up debris along their path of the walk. This is an efficient way of picking up an area in a quick easy and organized fashion. All the volunteers stick together and clean the same areas. No volunteers should go alone; always ensure they are in a buddy pair. If your volunteers split up to pick up trash, have a sign in sheet to ensure all volunteers are accounted for at the end of their clean up shifts.

FOD (Foreign Object Debris) LINE

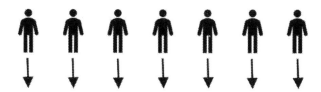

The essential items needed for clean-up activity and the amount is dependent on the number of volunteers participating.

- ☐ Trash bags
- ☐ Gloves
- ☐ Antibacterial wipes
- ☐ Water
- ☐ Gatorade
- ☐ Sunscreen
- ☐ Bug Spray
- ☐ First Aid Kit
- ☐ Sign in / Sign out sheet

CHAPTER 4

Military Appreciation

It had been brought to my attention that our city had a newly formed nonprofit whose mission is to house homeless veterans in a residential home while they assist in their positive reintegration back into society. All too often with the aftermath of returning from war, veterans find themselves facing Post Traumatic Stress Disorder (PTSD). According to the www.va.gov website, Post Traumatic Stress Disorder is a disorder that develops in some people who have experienced a shocking, scary, or dangerous event. As a result of PTSD and its effects to the brain and body, the veteran can end up losing their marriage, children, income, and lastly, their means of food and shelter if not properly diagnosed and treated. According to www.va.gov, the US Department of

Veteran Affairs 2014 study concluded, twenty veterans commit suicide every day as a result of PTSD. PTSD often happens to service members serving overseas in war and conflict. The mental effects often result in the veteran's inability to return to their daily lives with ease. My husband who served over 20 years in the Airforce, now a retired military member, felt the critical need for us to support this nonprofit.

This nonprofit begins by helping the veteran apply for a copy of their birth certificate and acquire an identification card, so they can start the job-hunting process. No business considers you for employment without two forms of identification. A very critical detail which prevents individuals from even looking for lawful employment – especially if the individual is homeless. While going through their program, the veteran can stay in the residential home for 30 days while searching for a job and beginning to save money. Once they are ready to "graduate" from the house, the organization helps them to obtain a lease for an apartment. They also assist the veteran in furnishing the apartment with a bed, couch, kitchen appliances, and other house hold items which are all donations from the community. As I was learning more and more about their efforts, I was seeing a way we could help! People's hearts are warm and giving. People love to donate to a good cause especially when they know they are donating to someone specific and it's going for immediate and impactful use. This was a great Pay It Forward event in the making.

Fourth of July was around the corner! What a fantastic time to organize a celebration in their honor. We would show our appreciation by serving lunch and bringing household items as donations. Our volunteers knocked it out of the park with donations such as; a recliner chair, microwave, exercise equipment, brooms, shovels, bedding, pots, pans, bath towels, paper towels, toilet paper, tooth brushes, tooth paste, bath soap, laundry soap, canned goods, coffee, tea, spices, crackers, peanuts, and the list goes on and on. In addition to the donations, we wanted to leave them with a memento of our lunch to always remind them that even strangers appreciate their sacrifice and dedication -encouraging them to never lose hope and keep one foot in front of the other. I searched the internet for the perfect "Thank You" sign, printed it off, and framed each one. This would be their first personalized décor they could display in their new home to recall this day. Always serving as a reminder to them to never lose hope. Even when times get tough remember, strangers do care.

Below are some ways of giving back to the military in your community.

Welcoming Committee:

Join the military base welcoming committee to welcome new families moving to the base. The adjustment for military families can be difficult at times traveling to new locations. If your base does not have a welcoming committee, then consider creating one for your squadron. This committee can help acclimate the new members to the community and share area attractions, churches, schools, kid's organizations, recreations, restaurants, babysitters, mechanics, hair salons, and things to know about the city. One easy place to start is to think about what was important to you when you moved to the new base? What tidbits of information of the local area would be good to pass on?

Thank you and Recognition:

Acknowledging and thanking a military member for their service is simple, easy, and priceless. Extending gratitude for their service is important to acknowledge and shows appreciation. Active duty men and women sacrifice being away from their families for often months, if not years, at a time. They are separated from family and putting their lives on the line to protect our country. If you see a military member in uniform, a simple smile and thank you for your service will go a long way. If you feel so inclined, reach your hand out to further show your gratitude with a handshake or a hug.

Military Spousal Support:

While a military member goes on deployment, do not forget about the family he or she leaves behind. The spouse left behind is usually playing dual roles of parenting, housework, parental responsibilities, and all normal day to day activities which was previously split by the couple. One could lend support to the spouse of the deployed by offering to cook meals, babysit the children so the parent can run errands, invite the family over for dinner, help with household or mechanic repairs, mow the grass in the summer, take animals to vet appointments, or help feed and take care of animals just to name a few.

Care Packages to Deployed:

Collecting a list of items to send overseas to the deployed military is a great way to show appreciation for their sacrifice while away from their family and country. Often times, while being deployed they are limited to a small selection of items and appreciate the basic things from home.

Below are items that could be included in care packages. Please reference your local Post Office for guidelines and restrictions for the country you are sending your package to.

- ☐ Beef jerky
- ☐ Sunflower seeds
- ☐ Dried fruit
- ☐ Trail mix
- ☐ Granola bars
- ☐ Instant oatmeal

- ☐ Crackers
- ☐ Coffee
- ☐ Tea
- ☐ Drink mix (powder form)
- ☐ Pop tarts
- ☐ Rice Krispy treats
- ☐ Candy
- ☐ Cookies
- ☐ Popcorn
- ☐ Spices
- ☐ Gum
- ☐ Chap stick
- ☐ Soap
- ☐ Homemade greeting cards
- ☐ Puzzle books
- ☐ Card games

Gratitude Cards:

Holidays can be the hardest when away from your family and friends. Getting a group together to make gratitude cards for your local deployed military during the holidays is a very low cost and heartfelt act of kindness. Any major holidays where there is a celebration would be a good time to show your appreciation with a simple thank you card. If you or someone you know, knows a deployed military member overseas this makes it easier for direct shipment to the person. If you do not know a person to send them to then deliver the cards to your local military branch for them to send overseas.

Visit your local VA (Veteran's Affairs) Medical Center, Transitional Living Center (TLC):

TLC provides veterans with the opportunity to receive care while working to increase their quality of life. They are housed in the VA Medical Center and depending on their specific circumstance they are nursed back to maximum health potential or to end of life care. There are several easy ways to encourage and show support. Attend their weekly Bingo game, read a book to them, donate time to help with their meal feeding, visit them, and listen to their stories and history. For more information, regarding VA and TLC can be found on www.va.gov.

Homeless Vets Outreach:

If your community has a local nonprofit who supports homeless Veteran's reintegration into society, reach out and inquire what donations or services are required. Often times they accept donations such as furniture, gently used household goods, toiletries, bicycles, or services such as job hunting, resume writing, and financial assistance. Your local VA or United Way can advise if your community supports a homeless veteran nonprofit. To find out if you have one in your community, contact your local VA or United Way, www.va.gov or www. unitedway.org.

At any time, you can reach out to your local military base to inquire how to support them and their causes.

CHAPTER 5

Senior Care Appreciation

Our Pay It Forward event was at a retirement home in an effort to spice up their weekly bingo game the residents participated in on a weekly basis. Going into the volunteer opportunity I was not prepared for the important life lesson I was going to learn that day. I went about my business planning, organizing, and ensuring we had enough volunteers (both of adult age and youth), quality prizes and delicious finger type pastries to serve the residents. Our intent going into the day was to make them feel celebrated. The event went off without a hitch and everyone was having a delightful time. The junior volunteers were embracing their roles acting as waitstaff during the bingo games by replenishing the brownies, cookies, and pastries and refilling the beverages. It was a successful event! Smiles beamed on everyone's faces, from the residents to the volunteers.

As we were tidying up the area before we left, the residents mingled with the volunteers thanking them for the memorable event. One resident came up close to me and whispered, "You know, I may not be here the next time you come back to visit. Please know how much we appreciate your group spending time with us. This has really been a lovely change from our normal routine." Wow, I tried to make light of her comment to ease my own uncomfortableness and said, "Oh now, you will most definitely be here the next time and I look forward to seeing you!" However, it made me stop and think for a minute. She had reached a point in her life where her day to day life perspective was just that - I might not be living the next time. While she was one of the fortunate ones who had lived out her life to its fullest, this was something we all should consider. Appreciate each day on purpose as though it's your last. Live each day with a heart filled with love and gratitude for each waking moment because life has no guarantees.

As we were cleaning up after the event, the only items we had remaining were the balloons. I had looked to one of our volunteers and asked him to hand out the balloons to our junior volunteers who participated. He then posed a question I hadn't considered. He said, "Why not let the residents take them back to their room?" I had a rather humorous look about my face and said, "You really think they would want one?" He said, "Sure, let's ask." As we approached the residents and inquired if they'd like to take a balloon back to their room their faces lit up with excitement. They exclaimed, "We would love to take one back to our rooms!" So, they did. The residents tied a single red or blue balloon to their walkers and with immense delight they went about their way returning to their rooms. This was so interesting to me.

The life lesson I learned in that moment was humbling and significant. As we grow older we forget to stop and enjoy the simple things in life which use to bring us joy. The air we breathe, shelter over our heads, a full belly after a delicious home cooked meal, reading a good book, the beauty of a single flower in bloom, or in this case, the youthfulness of a balloon. My 3-year-old nephews who were also at the event, enjoyed the balloons as much as the elderly residents did. What did they understand what the rest of us had forgotten? As we grow into adulthood the seriousness and burdens we put on ourselves to conform to the pressures of the world instantly cloud our vision. Long hours put in at the office, hustling to get everything accomplished on our "to-do" lists in the end don't amount to much. They are not nearly as important as who you want surrounding you in the end; family, friends, and loved ones. We overlook the simple things in life we used to appreciate in place of getting ahead and keeping up with life's ever-increasing expectations. This was a great reminder for me to find the joys in each moment. Not to get too caught up in the overwhelming expectations of life that cause us to overlook life's roses or in this case the balloons along the way.

Each morning if we have the privilege of waking up it should be considered a gift. It's important we say thank you and this gift not be taken for granted. For one day we will look back and wonder where has the time gone. I want to ensure I spend my time with meaning and purpose. And never let a day go by where those I treasure so dearly don't forget how much they are loved.

Below are some ways you can spend time at a Senior Care center and spread kindness.

Spice Up Bingo:

Call your local Senior Center and find out when is their next Bingo game. It's important to ask if someone from their facility will continue to run the Bingo game or if they want your group to run the game. If they would like you to, take time to familiarize yourself with their Bingo operations ahead of time. Coordinate with friends to add a little extra zest to their game. Bring prizes for the winners such as puzzle books, soft candy, scarves, coffee mugs, blank greeting cards, bracelets, and scratch off lottery tickets. Baked goodies and decorations such as balloons can add to the occasion. Also, inquire the average age of the residents and have a playlist with songs during that era. If there is a holiday coming up, make it a holiday themed Bingo game.

Sharing your Talent:

If you have a talent for singing, cooking, or making crafts consider sharing your talents with the residents. Bake mini loaves of bread or treats or if you are crafty, make small crafts for each of their rooms for a holiday or just because. The Coordinator of Activities for the Senior Center can even provide information on scheduled classes so you can attend or better yet maybe lead a class. If your talent is your voice, offer to sing while they are eating or having an activity.

Donate your Time:

Your family and children can donate time and read a book to the residents, individually or in a group setting. This is a wonderful activity to do as a family or with your children and costs nothing but your time.

Kindness Notes:

One easy way to pay it forward is to leave random kindness notes throughout the facility. This can be done with your family, with children, a group of friends or even just by yourself. Once you have made the notes, go to the Reception Desk and tell them you'd like to leave these for the residents. They will no doubt honor your request to walk through the facility or even help by giving you suggestions on how to sprinkle the notes.

CHAPTER 6

Natural Disaster Relief

In 2017, Hurricane Harvey devastated Texas by swallowing up the Houston area and left so many without power, clothing, shelter, and destroyed many childhood homes. As my son and I watched the devastation unfold on the television from our living room in Kansas, we were in sheer terror watching people be carried out of their homes in waste deep water while children were screaming for their mothers and fathers. My 10-year-old son was clearly moved as he sat in utter silence mesmerized by what he was seeing on the television screen. I said aloud, mostly to myself, "I wish there was some way to help." Not realizing my son was listening he said, "Yes! Me too, how can we help?" Unfortunately, at that time I wasn't sure of a hands-on way we could help other than sending money to Red Cross.

Only a few days later while mindlessly scrolling through Facebook, I came across a post that caught my eye. A local non-profit in our city was gathering donations to send to a shelter in the Houston area to help the victims. They were directly connected to a shelter in Houston and our donations would be sent to help them. I was elated! This is what we needed to do as a family. We were continuing to see footage on television of the aftermath of the hurricane and they were in dire need of help. This was a perfect opportunity for us to provide support. I printed out the items the shelter was requesting and anxiously waited for my son to arrive home from school.

At dinner, I explained to my husband and son that I learned of a way we could help the victims of hurricane Harvey. A local non-profit in our city was collecting supplies for Houston. They had provided a list of household items, hygiene and other medical supplies that they were in desperate need of. My son's face lit up. He asked, "Can I help pick out the items to donate?"

"Absolutely!" I said. We would make it a family affair and take a trip to our local Walmart after dinner. I handed the list to my son and a $10 bill. This was also a prime opportunity to teach him the value of a dollar and how fast it can be spent. He carefully selected each item with care and my husband helped him keep track of the price; toothbrush, toothpaste, soap, and hairbrushes. He said, "Wow this doesn't seem like enough, but I know they will appreciate it." He was right, they would greatly appreciate it even something as simple as a toothbrush. This has been a valuable experience for my son. He was exposed to what life is about, helping others in need as well as the value of a dollar.

When you see natural disasters in the world it can often provide feelings of helplessness. You want to lend support in some way but have no idea where to start. Organizational relief drives are often formed after a team of people or non-profits come together to access the situation and communicate the request for supplies and assistance needed. Below are ideas on how you can jump in and be of assistance to organizations who assist with natural disasters.

Church Relief:

Reach out to your local church organizations. Often times, church organizations contact local churches in the impacted area and pull together a team of people to travel to the disaster site to help with boots on the ground. Check your local churches, news stations, or on social media to see who in your area is traveling to the disaster site to offer help. Do not take it upon yourself to drive to the disaster site alone. This could put you in harm's way and also hinder what relief remedies are taking place. It's best to go with an organization who has been given the green light and invited to come help for a specific location and cause.

Donation Drive:

In the event of a natural disaster, your family or community can join together and collect donation items for the victims. Crisis situations often leave people without the basic necessities to function in their day to day lives. Coordinating a drive to collect the essential items can be helpful to bridge the time between when the victims receive permanent help from shelters or resume their daily routines.

Area Shelter Donations:

Reaching out to area shelters to see what items they need is also a fantastic way to help during times of crisis. Once you have a list of items to support the needs of the shelter, you can begin collecting in your community. United Way is also an excellent resource for times of need. Your area United Way can provide a resource guide with numbers of local non-profits for you to reach out to directly and request items they are needing for donation. www.unitedway.org

Donate to Organization Campaigns:

The Red Cross asks for donations of blood, volunteering your time, and money in times of crisis. www.redcross. org. Also, Go Fund Me fundraisers are set up in honor of the disaster. In which case, money can be donated to help the local community purchase water, essentials and hygiene items. Visit the Go Fund Me page to inquire about fundraisers for the disaster. www.gofundme.com.

If you choose to donate money to an organization assisting in the disaster sites, inquire where the funds will go. Research different organizations and see how they allocate their donation resources. Often times administrative fees are taken out and not always 100% of the donations go directly to the area in need. If you want to donate to an organization to help support relief efforts, first do some research until you find the one you are most comfortable donating to.

PART 2

KINDNESS CHALLENGE

CHAPTER 7

Children's Kindness Challenge

I've been retired now for about 15 years and while I enjoy my days taking in a round of golf with my buddies, yard work, and tinkering in the garage, I wanted to do something to give back to MY community. So, I began a side hobby of repairing used bicycles and donating them to young children in need.

My new hobby started out with about 12 bicycles which had been generously given to me from area businesses. They were of all different sizes and I began working to repair and restore them. One night my wife and I were at a restaurant which we are regulars at, and while eating dinner I began talking to the waitress about my new hobby. I asked her if she knew any kids that were in need of a bicycle. She said she did not, however, her daughter is a school counselor and she would check with her. I gave her my phone number and told her to reach out to me in the event her daughter came across someone in need.

Within 24 hours my phone rang. It was the waitress from the restaurant. She had spoken with her daughter and there was an immediate need of a bicycle for a young 8-year-old boy. She said he was late to school in the mornings on a regular basis because he was walking upwards of 2 miles to school every day. Winter and freezing temperatures were just around the corner, so time was of the essence.

I went to the third bay of my garage to find the perfect bicycle for the little boy. The trouble was none of them were in pristine condition. I knew this little boy needed the best. He had been enduring what most kids only hear about. Most kids hear stories from their parents of walking miles and miles, uphill, through the snow to get to school. Only this young boy was actually doing just that. Walking to school, in whatever the Kansas weather conditions were for the day; hot sun, pouring rain, straight line winds, or bitter cold snow. Since the young boy needed transportation immediately, I delivered the best bicycle for his size I had at the time. I knew this would work temporarily until I could get him the exceptional bike he so deserved.

A few weeks went by, and I was able to find the Cadillac version for this little boy. I gave it to his Mom and told her he could keep the original one also. Thinking maybe he had a brother he could pass on the original bike to as he grew older.

Several weeks had passed and I received a call from the little boy's mother. She wanted my address because her son had something he wanted to send me. In talking with her, I asked how he was doing and she informed me he passed on the original bike I had given him to a friend who was also in desperate need of a bicycle. Another little boy just like him who was walking to school every day. My heart was filled with joy. Another child was blessed by the donation. Now the two boys were able to ride their bikes side by side together to school. Without even knowing what he'd done just by acting from the heart, the little boy had paid it forward to a friend. The good fortune he'd received from an anonymous stranger, who just wanted to give a gift of a bicycle, in turn the boy had done the same for his friend. What an amazing ripple effect of love in motion.

The experiences children have while growing up often mold who they are and continue to shape their characteristics as they grow into adulthood. If they experience feelings of kindness, compassion and giving when they are young, and those feelings inhabit warmth and love inside, the hope is they continue to replicate those feelings into their permanent characteristics as they grow older. Instilling the exercise of spreading acts of kindness at a young age teaches children the importance of love, grace, and acceptance. Qualities that can't be taught in school but more in living life through compassionate experiences.

Below are ideas on how to incorporate Pay It Forward ideas for your children. They can be done as Monthly

Challenges where you challenge everyone in the family to do one act of kindness every day for a month, or a Weekend Challenge where your family dedicates one weekend a month to do random acts of kindness. Start incorporating kindness activities and you just might find it fosters a loving and merciful atmosphere in your household and in your children's hearts.

Pay it Forward ideas for Children:

- Homemade kindness cards for senior care center
- Bake cookies and give to neighbors, family, or friends
- Use sidewalk chalk to write messages for strangers
- Take flowers or fresh fruit to your teacher as a thank you
- Give your teacher a thank you note
- Share toys with siblings or friends
- Donate unused toys to families in need
- Donate socks and gloves to a homeless shelter
- Donate clothes you have outgrown to a younger child in need
- Start a Little Free Library in your neighborhood

- Play with a new kid on the playground
- Sit with someone at lunch who is sitting alone
- Help another kid with his homework
- Leave random post it notes telling someone to have an awesome day
- Leave a kind note in a library book
- Go to your local park and feed the birds
- Pick up trash in your neighborhood and/or community
- Volunteer at your local animal shelter
- Adopt an animal from the Humane Society
- Help neighborhood pets/animals return home by checking their tag and calling the owners
- Help your sibling do chores
- Help your parents make dinner
- Do your chores without being asked
- Pick up your toys without being asked
- Donate stuffed animals to your local children's hospital
- Help your neighbors rake leaves
- If your neighbor's newspaper is at the end of the driveway, deliver it to their porch

- Volunteer to feed your neighbor's pets while they are away on vacation
- Offer to water your neighbor's plants while they are away on vacation
- Offer to pick up your neighbor's mail while they are away on vacation
- Give your bike to a younger kid who doesn't have one
- Collect donations for families impacted by natural disasters
- Donate profits from your Lemonade stand to a community cause or family in need
- Pick a family off the Angel Tree at Christmas to buy presents for during the holidays

CHAPTER 8

Personal Kindness Challenge

My favorite personal challenge story happened with my mom and one of her closest friends, Cindy. The story gives both ladies goosebumps to this day. I must be honest, I get them as well, but not because it happened to me, but for the layers upon layers of lessons that are found within the experience. Here is her story.

Being raised a Catholic, Lent always brought thoughts of no meat Fridays and giving up that special thing you couldn't live without; candy, soda, movies during the time before Easter. Those were pretty easy for me at that time, because we were pretty poor and really didn't get those extras very often anyway. But I thought, I was checking that box as a Catholic.

As I grew older, no longer a practicing Catholic, the sacrifice or practice of giving up something during Lent stayed with me. The abstinence remained in my makeup. Even though I'm older now, the thinking of giving up my cookies, chips, or now a glass of wine was good and, oh by the way, I could benefit myself by losing a few pounds. So, a win-win.

This year, I have really been introduced to the Pay It Forward concept because of my daughter and son-in-law. Their unselfish giving has really presented me with the true meaning of paying it forward. So, as Lent approached, my usual surrendering did not seem to fit the true meaning of what Lent is or what paying it forward was supposed to mean. The sacrifices I thought I was making in the past were really pretty selfish on my part.

While deciding what to do this Lent, I tried to think more along the lines of truly paying it forward. One of my, what I use to call "give ups" was actually going to be a "give to" (someone else). I decided besides my usual little acts of kindness I do now, I would do one large (for me, that is) act of kindness a week.

Week one came to me immediately. I watch garage sales on Facebook daily; a lady wanting to buy a swing costing $40 listed said she only had $20 until the weekend. She asked if the seller could hold it until then. I only had a $20 in my purse but knew immediately it was meant to be given away. I messaged the seller, told her I would pay the other $20. We met and my $20 was given for a good cause. The lady picked up her swing and never knew who paid the other half of the $40.

Week two came to me as I was sitting in the Taco Bell drive thru. I drove to the window to pay and pick up my order. I heard the person behind me ordering and the cashier tells them that their bill was $3.20. Sweet, I could handle this one, no sweat. I gave the lady my $10, paid for my food, and the one behind me and even got change back. The cashier told me that she just loved when people paid it forward like that. Driving home, I have to admit, I felt pretty proud of myself.

Week three, it was Friday afternoon as I was driving to meet a friend for lunch and pick up a "to go order" at the same restaurant for a party my husband and I were going to that night and I just happened to remember I had not done my "pay it forward" for the week. Trying to think of what I could do, knowing I really didn't have plans to go nor do anything that would provide me with an opportunity to do my weeks' pay it forward, I pondered on a few things. Nothing came to mind and as I drove into the parking lot of the restaurant, my mind quickly raced to what I was going to eat for lunch, if my friend was already there, if the place was busy. The unusual nonsense thoughts that fill your mind as you walk into any restaurant.

I walked in, the restaurant was not too busy, noon rush was over, my friend was not there, whew, so I had time to check my phone. As I sat there, our waitress brought a glass of water and told me the specials of the day. I told her I was waiting on a friend and would order when she came. I couldn't help but notice a gentleman that sat down beside me in the next booth. My mind quickly went to the thoughts of; I wonder how he could afford to eat here. Although, he didn't look homeless, he didn't really look like the kind of person that would frequent this type of restaurant. His clothes were shabby, not with holes, but not real neat. I looked his way and smiled; he looked my way and nodded. My friend soon came and we were busily catching up on what has been going on in each other's lives as the waitress came for our order. I had decided on the special of the day, salmon with herb topping. While my friend was ordering, I quickly looked over to the man sitting next to us to see what he had ordered. As he looked at me, looking at his plate, I told him, "I was checking to see if you ordered the salmon, I wanted to see what it looked like". He smiled and we both said chicken at the same time. I smiled and quickly looked at the waitress and gave her my order. Still wondering to myself, how this man was eating here.

As we were eating, talking and enjoying each other's company, the cashier brought my order to go and told me how to warm it when I got it home. Neither one of us noticed as the gentleman sitting next to us got up to leave, but I did see him at the cashiers' desk. He seemed to know the cashier and the workers behind the counter.

So much so, I remember thinking, he must come here often.

As soon as he left, both the owner and the cashier came running to our table. I didn't think much of it as the owner knows my friend well. As they came to our table with huge smiles on their faces, they exclaimed, he paid your entire bill!! We both looked in surprise and together said "WHAT?" at the same time. He paid the entire bill, over $100 in cash. Our mouths dropped open. My stomach, in fact, my whole body started getting butterflies. I was crying inside, smiling inside and tears were filling both our eyes. "What's his name" What's his number?" my friend and I asked. They both said, "We don't know, he paid in cash." He has only been here one other time, so we don't know him at all.

My butterflies continued for seconds which seemed like minutes. In my mind, I kept wondering if he was a God Wink given to me to show me how selfish my giving really is. My friend was overwhelmed too. She kept saying, I don't know what to say." I think we need to pay him back, but how?

I am sure she and I will continue to try to think of a way to pay back what a tremendous feeling this unknown friend gave to us that day. To know what a person feels like who receives a true "pay it forward" from the heart, will forever live in my heart and soul. Trust me, I have had one of those special people give me that unforgettable gift that only a "receiver" can feel. I know his gift was from his heart even though he said nothing and didn't even look back as he walked out of the restaurant. I only hope my gifts will give the same feelings of warmth to someone who will pass that feeling on to someone else and that person to someone else and so on.

One way to infuse a deep-seated happiness in your own life is by practicing daily gratitude and random acts of kindness regularly. When you begin your morning with a mission to seek out ways to help others, your view on the world changes. You make it a habit to look for ways you can help others and bring sunlight into their day. How you leave them sets an impression on their day, week and even their life. Make it your goal to only leave positive and loving imprints on those around you.

This next section provides a list of ideas on ways to spread kindness to people in your life you encounter daily. Start by setting a goal to do one pay it forward act a week. Once you have accomplished that goal, then progress to one a day and so on. After your act of kindness, reflect how it made you feel. What response did you get from the recipient? How did it make the person feel? Were those around you surprised or taken back by the act of kindness too? It's important to acknowledge the affect you have because you better understand the magnitude of your actions. Therefore, realizing all actions have a ripple effect whether they are positive or not.

Pay it Forward ideas for individuals in your family:

- Call your parents – just because
- Thank your parents
- Acknowledge your siblings and tell them how much you appreciate them
- Acknowledge birthdays not just on social media (Facebook, Twitter, etc.)
- Inquire how they are doing – and listen
- Support your nieces/nephews/cousin's fundraisers

- Support your nieces/nephews/cousin by attending a game they are playing in
- Send a random text letting them know you are thinking of them

Pay it Forward ideas for your spouse or significant other:

- Make surprise dinner plans
- Be the first to apologize
- Write your partner a list of things you love about them
- Give your partner the benefit of the doubt
- Acknowledge your partner when they help around the house
- Help take out the trash/do the dishes/finish the laundry – even if it's not your turn
- Give your partner a hug first thing when you get home
- Go to bed the same time as your partner
- Hold your partner's hand
- Leave a surprise sticky note in their lunch bag – letting them know you are thinking of them

- Just do it! Whatever it is, without them having to ask
- Tell your partner's parents how much you appreciate their son/daughter
- Buy a small gift just to say "I am thinking of you"
- Send a surprise email or text saying "You are thinking of them"
- Ask how you can help with a project they are doing
- As their birthday approaches pay closer attention, so you don't have to ask them what they want for a present ... you will know!

Pay it Forward ideas for your friends:

- Call/Text a friend "just because" and tell them you are thinking of them
- Support friends by attending their events
- Take a friend out for coffee if they are going through a tough time
- Give a friend a book you think they would enjoy
- Refer a friend's service to others

- Leave a nice compliment on a friend's fb/twitter posts
- Share friend's social media posts
- Go to your friend's children's events

Pay it Forward ideas for your coworkers:

- Smile and be cheerful
- Make a new pot of coffee; or Refill the Krueg water
- Reload the copy machine with paper
- Organize a potluck or lunch gathering to socialize with co-workers
- Give up your close parking space to someone
- Clean the community refrigerator
- Bake fresh cookies or treat for the office
- Bring in fresh veggies from the garden

Pay it Forward ideas for random shoppers:

- Let someone with a smaller purchase go in front of you in the checkout line
- Returning your own shopping cart to return place or inside store

- While you are returning your shopping cart, return another person's as well
- Pay for a stranger's groceries
- Help bag your own groceries (when possible)
- Sign up your grocery store Plus card to donate $ to a local non-profit
- Be a courtesy shopper
- Say "yes" to the cashier when asked if you want to donate $1 for a specific cause

Pay it Forward ideas for anyone:

- Smile at strangers
- Pay for a stranger's bus/train pass
- Pay for a stranger's expired parking meter
- Pick up trash along the city streets/parks
- Offer a homeless person your leftovers
- Donate clothes to the homeless shelters
- Pay for parking pass for the car behind you
- Leave a nice tip to your server
- Compliment a stranger
- Be present – put your phone down when talking to someone

- Be a courteous driver - let someone merge into your lane.
- Give someone a hug
- Leave sticky notes with positive slogans in random places
- Send anonymous card or flowers to someone
- Adopt a rescue pet
- Selflessly help (promote) others
- Write a thank you letter to someone who has made a difference in your life
- Bring someone home a souvenir from a vacation
- Deliver or order flowers for someone
- Fill someone's car up with gas
- Invite someone over for the holidays
- Knit a scarf or blanket for someone
- Pay the toll for the car behind you
- Pay for the car behind you in the drive thru line
- Hold the door open for someone

APPENDIX

Event agendas are vital in communicating all the important information to your participants. Where they need to be, when they need to be there, and what items to bring, will help your event be successful. The form in the appendix is an example. Microsoft Word has numerous templates you can refer to and customize to fit your needs.

A Volunteer Sign Up Form is important for several reasons. It's a helpful aid in tracking the attendance of those volunteering at your outreach activity. Plus, it's critical to keep track of your volunteers to ensure everyone has departed your event safely. It's also a useful reference for thank you notes or to reach out for feedback on how to improve your activities for the next time.

A Volunteer Waiver form is a valuable tool to use for events with volunteers. A waiver form is used to protect event sponsors from any liability due to any injury suffered by participants. Release forms can be enlightening making people think about the possible risks of an activity. An easy site for you to create your event waiver form is at www.formswift.com. A small fee will allow you to customize the forms for your specific events.

These are some helpful tools to ease the planning and organizing of your event. Depending on the complexity of your activity, a budget sheet or event planning guide can also be beneficial. Microsoft Word supplies many templates to provide a starting point for planning.

EVENT AGENDA

Event Title:	Date of Event:
Location (Address):	Start Time – End Time:
Event Coordinator: (Focal Name / Phone Number)	
Items to Bring: (Supplies List)	
Attendees: (Volunteer list)	
EVENT DETAILS	
Activity; Start Time – End Time	Location
Activity; Start Time – End Time	Location
Activity; Start Time – End Time	Location
Activity; Start Time – End Time	Location
Activity; Start Time – End Time	Location

Additional Instructions:

Use this section for additional instructions, comments, or directions.

PAY IT FOWARD
VOLUNTEER SIGN UP SHEET

VOLUNTEER NAME	PHONE NUMBER	EMAIL ADDRESS	SIGN IN TIME	SIGN OUT TIME

Additional Instructions:

Use this section for additional instructions, comments, or directions.

ACKNOWLEDGEMENT

I would like to thank my editor Heather McChesney for her literary expertise and guidance in composing this manuscript. You were unquestionably instrumental in the crafting of this book. To my Mom, Dad and Husband who contributed with your stories, thank you for allowing me to share; Much love and blessings to each of you.

ABOUT THE AUTHOR

Kristi Arno and her husband are the Founders of Pay It Forward Hearts Foundation. This Kansas based non-profit's vision, "together we can change the world" has a heartfelt mission to "help people feel a glimpse of hope by sprinkling love, grace and kindness to others." She inspires others by using her compassion and positivity to encourage a daily pay it forward way of life so everyone is touched by kindness and generosity. She believes if we join together, we can infuse more love into the world one random act of kindness at a time.

Printed in the United States
By Bookmasters